BARBARA
JORDAN

Congresswoman

by
Linda Carlson Johnson

A BLACKBIRCH PRESS BOOK

WOODBRIDGE, CONNECTICUT

Published by Blackbirch Press, Inc.
260 Amity Road
Woodbridge, CT 06525

©1990 Blackbirch Press, Inc.
First Edition

Printed in Hong Kong

10 9 8 7 6 5 4 3

Library of Congress Cataloging-in-Publication Data

Johnson, Linda Carlson, 1949-
    Barbara Jordan, congresswoman/by Linda Carlson Johnson.—1st
ed.
        p.   cm. — (The Library of famous women)
    Includes bibliographical references and index.
    Summary: Surveys the life and career of the black woman from Texas
who became a lawyer, state legislator, and member of the United States
Congress.
    ISBN 1-56711-031-2   ISBN 1-56711-050-9 (softcover)
    1. Jordan, Barbara, 1936-   —Juvenile literature. 2. Legislators—
United States—Biography—Juvenile literature. 3. United States. Congress.
House—Biography—Juvenile literature. [1. Jordan, Barbara, 1936-
2. Legislators. 3. Afro-Americans—Biography.] I. Title. II. Series.
E840.8.J62J64 1990
328.73'092—dc20   90-40026
 [B]   CIP
                                        AC

Contents

Introduction

Barbara Jordan may not be a name you know. But Barbara Jordan is a person you should meet. She is an important American woman.

United States capitol in Washington, D.C.

(*Left*)
Barbara Jordan—lawyer, congresswoman, and college professor.

When Barbara was born on February 21, 1936, she didn't have much going for her. She was black in a time when black people were expected to "keep their place." She was a girl in a time when men had all the power in the United States. And she was poor.

But Barbara Jordan didn't think of herself as a poor black girl. Barbara's parents taught her to expect the best of herself. And Barbara had two great gifts—an amazing mind and a powerful voice. She used her gifts to become a lawyer, a state senator, a member of the U.S. Congress, and a college teacher. She also became an American hero.

This book is Barbara Jordan's story.

Chapter 1

Neighborhood and Family

Houston, Texas, around 1936.

Houston, Texas, around 1936.

Little Barbara Jordan's world wasn't very big. She lived in an all-black neighborhood in Houston, Texas. The streets were lined with flowering trees and well-kept houses with neatly mowed lawns, but the people were poor.

Barbara didn't think of her family as poor because she knew no other way of life. "We were all black and we were all poor and we were all right there in the same place," Barbara said later.

Houston in 1936

When Barbara Jordan was born in 1936, black people in Houston didn't have much choice about where they lived or the kind of jobs they had. The black people in Houston, who were then called Negroes, lived in all-black sections of town. Some of these sections were next to all-white neighborhoods. Many black people worked during the day as servants or maids in the white parts of town, then they went home to their own neighborhoods. Black kids went to school in their neighborhoods, and white kids went to school in their neighborhoods. Many black children had never even seen a white child.

When black people did go into the white sections of town, there were special rules they had to follow. On buses, for example, black people had to sit in the back. And if a bus was crowded, the black people were expected to stand so that the white people on the bus could sit down. Black people couldn't eat in the same restaurants as white people could. Black people couldn't even use the same bathrooms and water fountains. There were signs on restroom doors and over water fountains that said "Whites Only" or "Coloreds Only." (*Colored* was another word that was used in those times to describe black people.)

Growing Up a Jordan

Ben Jordan, Barbara's father, knew that Houston wasn't the only place where things were hard for blacks. He knew that all through the southern part of the United States, black people were treated

Blacks in the South had only small buildings like this one to use for their churches.

the same way they were treated in Houston. And even in the northern part of the United States, Ben knew, it wasn't easy for black people to get good jobs.

But when Ben Jordan talked to his girls, Bennie, Rose Mary, and Barbara, he didn't talk to them about how hard life would be for them. He talked instead about how important it was for them to get a good education. And he taught them that if they worked hard enough, they would succeed at anything they tried to do. He always told his girls, "No man can take away your brain."

Both Ben and Arlyne, Barbara's mother, were very smart, and they knew how to speak well. They knew their daughters were smart too, so they expected their girls to use words well and learn to say exactly what they thought.

When Barbara was about 12, her father became a Baptist minister. The job didn't pay very much, so he had to keep his job working in a warehouse. But because he was a minister, Ben became a leader in the black community. In the black neighborhoods, church was the one place where people could express themselves freely and openly.

Sunday at Good Hope

Even before Ben Jordan became a minister, Sunday was the most special day of the week for the Jordan family. Arlyne always made sure that she and her girls looked beautiful for church. First, there were baths for all the children. Then Arlyne spent time carefully combing and braiding the girls' hair and pressing their Sunday-best dresses. Once the girls were dressed, they were inspected to be sure they looked just right.

Then the family, which included Grandma and Grandpa Jordan, would pile into two big black cars, a Model T Ford and an Oldsmobile. They would head for the Good Hope Missionary Baptist Church. Charles Jordan, Barbara's grandfather, always opened the service by leading the first hymn. He would also pray for the preacher and for the people, asking Jesus to "ride on" with all of them at school, in the streets, and at home.

The church services at Good Hope Missionary Baptist Church often lasted for hours. People would read parts of the Bible out loud. Then the preacher would give his sermon. He would often preach for a long time, but he kept the people's

Many members of black churches would shout and throw their arms in the air during a sermon.

attention with the way he spoke. He would usually start by speaking very softly, then his voice would become louder and louder. Whenever the people felt strongly about something the preacher said, they would shout out things like "Jesus" and "Hallelujiah."

As Barbara grew older, she listened carefully to the rich voices of the preacher and the other people who spoke at Good Hope. It wasn't long before Barbara herself began to read poems and sing solos in church. The people came to love her rich, deep voice.

Barbara remembers the first day she listened to her father preach. She was filled with the sense of how right her father sounded as he spoke. She knew that Ben Jordan had to be a preacher, even though he still had to work in the warehouse to make enough money for the family. He had things to say to people about God.

Lessons from a Junk Man

Although Barbara enjoyed church, it was never her favorite part of Sunday. What she looked forward to most was the time she spent with her grandpa. He was a special person in her life. He made her feel important.

Every Sunday after church, the Jordans would go to Grandmother and Grandpa Patten's house for Sunday noon dinner. Soon after the meal, Bennie and Rose Mary would head back to church for youth meetings, and Barbara's parents would go home. But Barbara always stayed.

In the afternoons, she helped her Grandpa Patten with his business. He was a junk man. He had a cart and a horse that he would take around the white neighborhoods of Houston each week. The people would set out things for Mr. Patten to collect: rags, paper, metal, anything they didn't want anymore. On Sundays, Barbara helped her grandpa sort the rags and paper and metal into piles. Then a man would come to buy the junk by the pound. It was Barbara's job to weigh the piles carefully on the scale.

Barbara loved being part of something as grown-up as a business. Grandpa Patten always gave some of the money he made to Barbara. And he often bought her special things, such as bicycles. At one point, Barbara had three bicycles, all from her Grandpa Patten.

But Barbara didn't love her Grandpa Patten for the things he gave her. She loved him because of the kind of man he was and for the special way he treated her. Grandpa Patten always told Barbara how much he cared for her. He told her that he expected her to be different from all the other kids in the neighborhood. When he saw Barbara playing with kids that he thought were bad, he told Barbara not to do that anymore.

Sunday evenings with Grandpa Patten were even more special than the Sunday afternoons she spent in the junkyard with him. After the day's work was done, Grandpa Patten would go down the street to get an evening snack for the two of them to eat together. The owner of a local restaurant would give Grandpa Patten a big bagful of food when Grandpa Patten knocked at the back door of the restaurant. Black people were not allowed to come in the front door of the restaurant, which served only white people. The owner would give away barbecued rib and sausage ends because he couldn't serve them to his customers.

Grandpa Patten and Barbara loved the treat of barbecue on a Sunday night. And as they ate, they would talk. Most of what Barbara and Grandpa Patten talked about was the Bible and God. Barbara often said that she learned more about religion from Grandpa Patten than she ever learned in church.

Grandpa Patten had stopped going to church himself years before Barbara was born, but he still believed in the power of God. In red crayon, he would write his thoughts about parts of the Bible on scraps of paper. One lesson that Grandpa Patten found in the Bible was that the world is a schoolroom. He told Barbara that life was "not a holiday but an education." And the one lesson that everyone had to learn, Grandpa Patten said, was to learn better how to love.

Grandpa Patten also spent a lot of time during these talks with Barbara telling her about the life of Jesus. He told Barbara that she should follow the example of Jesus in her life. According to Grandpa Patten, one of the most important lessons from the life of Jesus was "Don't get sidetracked and be like everyone else."

One day, Barbara would understand that lesson. She would learn it so well that she would become a person who would play a special role in history. But she was still a young girl, and she had a lot yet to learn.

Chapter 2

School Days

Barbara enjoyed singing and dancing like other teenagers.

Barbara didn't realize that Grandpa Patten had great hopes for her. She just knew what a special man he was, and she knew that the lessons he had taught her were the right ones. In her heart, she had already decided that she would grow up to take a different, special path.

But as a young teenager, Barbara Jordan wanted to be like other teenagers. So she combed her hair under and wore scoop-neck dresses and rhinestone jewelry, just like all the other girls. She had slumber parties at her house and went to the ser-vicemen's club with her friends to meet guys. Sometimes, at the club, Barbara would get up and sing popular songs like "Money, Honey" for the crowd. At 14, she got her driver's license so she could take her friends out in her father's big car for hamburgers and shakes.

Being "Too Black"

Barbara had many friends. Some of them were friends from grade school, like the Justice sisters. All their lives, these girls had done just about everything together.

Barbara was accepted by everyone she knew. But when she got to Phyllis Wheatley High School, she found out that there was something about her that made her different from many of the other kids. Her skin was too black.

All the kids at Wheatley were black. In those days, there was no such thing as a school that had both black and white students. But even in an all-black school, the kids and teachers thought it was important to be as "white" as possible. It was so "cool" to be light-skinned that many kids used skin bleach to try to make their skin look lighter.

Barbara didn't even try skin bleach. It would have been no use. Her skin was darker than anyone's in the school. Many kids—and even some teachers—didn't treat her the same way as they treated other kids. So Barbara knew that she would never be chosen as homecoming queen or cheerleader. The girls who won those contests had to be popular, which meant they had to have light skin.

Barbara's Gifts

Even though Barbara wanted to fit in, she also remembered the things her father and grandfather had said. They told her to use her mind, to be different. Barbara joined the debate team in high school, and she began to find out that she had two special gifts: a powerful voice and an ability to make people believe in what she had to say.

The high school debate team traveled all over Texas to compete against students from other schools. Barbara was a star. She knew just how to use her deep, rich, powerful voice to make her words sound important and right. She also knew how to make a good point in an argument. In high school, Barbara won two first-place awards in state debate contests and went on to speak in national contests.

In the first national contest, Barbara came in second. She learned from this experience that she didn't like to lose. In the second national contest, she won first place. She also won a $200 scholarship that she could use for college.

Barbara was pleased about the scholarship. She had known for a long time that she would go to college, just as her older sister Rose Mary had. Barbara also knew that she wanted to be a lawyer, though she wasn't exactly sure why.

Then, on Career Day, Barbara heard a woman lawyer speak. Edith Sampson stood tall and talked well. She seemed to be talking just to Barbara, telling her it was possible to be anything she wanted to be.

Barbara went home and told her parents that she wanted to be a lawyer. Her mother was against the idea. She didn't think it was right for a girl to become a lawyer. Both of Barbara's sisters wanted to be music teachers, and Mrs. Jordan thought that Barbara should choose to do something like that. Arlyne also thought that being a lawyer might keep her from getting married and raising a family. Arlyne believed these were the most important things a girl could do.

Ben Jordan disagreed with his wife. He was proud of Barbara, and he had known from the time she was a small girl that she had special gifts that she should use in special ways. He was glad that his daughter believed him when he said, "You can do whatever you want to do."

Chapter 3

College and Law School

Barbara was a natural leader and an eager student.

A $200 scholarship wasn't much of a start toward college. Barbara's family decided that she would have to go to a school close to home, at least for her first four years of college. By then, she might be able to afford to go to a good law school.

Choosing a college in the Houston area meant choosing an all-black college. Blacks and whites in the South still had to go to separate schools. Barbara chose to go to Texas Southern University and live at home.

Almost as soon as she arrived at college, Barbara began looking for a way to be a leader. She decided to be school president. Then she learned that a freshman was not allowed to run for president. So, once again, she joined the debate team.

The World Outside Texas

Barbara didn't join the team just to show off her speaking skills. She knew the team traveled to many other colleges to compete, and she wanted to see the rest of the United States.

That first trip Barbara took showed her the difference between the South and the North. In the South, the debate team coach had to plan trips very carefully because only certain motels would allow black people to stay. He also had to bring food along in the car because he couldn't count on finding a restaurant that would serve blacks. Often, the team couldn't even find a decent bathroom. At gas stations, the bathrooms were usually for white people only. The bathroom for "colored" people was often an outhouse in a field near the station.

Things were different in the North. In big cities such as Chicago, Boston, and New York, the students could eat in any restaurant they could afford. And they could stay in any motel where they could pay the price of the room.

Barbara had known that black people had few rights in the South. After all, she had lived there all her life. Everyone

When Barbara was a teenager, blacks were separated from whites in schools and even in public waiting rooms.

around her had accepted that life for black people and white people had to be different. In some ways, Barbara had accepted that too. But now she saw that, at least in some places, black people seemed to have more rights than they did in the South. And Barbara began to wonder what could be done to change things where she lived.

An Important Year for Black Rights

In 1954, when Barbara was a junior in college, the United States Supreme Court made an important decision. The Court said that as long as black children and white children were in separate schools, they could not get an equal education.

The judges ordered that black and white schools be mixed, or integrated, in the United States as soon as possible.

When Barbara heard about the Court decision, she thought things would change very quickly in Houston. She was wrong. In Houston, and in many other parts of the South, nothing changed in the schools. Barbara realized that if things were going to change in the South, black people would have to make them change.

The next year, 1955, a black woman in Alabama made a difference for black people. Her name was Rosa Parks. One day, Rosa got on a bus and decided to sit in a seat near the front, even though a state law in Alabama said black people had to sit in the back of the bus. When the bus driver told Rosa to move, she refused.

News of what Rosa had done spread throughout the South. Texas, like many other southern states, changed its laws so that black people no longer had to sit in the back of the bus.

Barbara wanted to make a difference, too. She didn't know quite what to do, but she wanted to be part of the struggle for black rights.

In 1955, Rosa Parks was arrested after she refused to move to the back of the bus.

In a small way, Barbara felt that the Texas Southern University debate team was helping in that struggle. The all-black team was often a surprise winner against teams from white schools. Barbara felt that she and the rest of the team were showing white Americans that black Americans could be their equals.

Law School — and Trouble

Barbara wanted to go to law school after she finished college. This time, she didn't want to go to an all-black school. She wanted to go to Harvard University, one of the best colleges in the country. Harvard didn't accept Barbara. It wasn't because her grades weren't good enough—they were. It wasn't because she was black—the school had already begun to accept black students. It was because she had gone to an all-black university in the South. Officials at Harvard didn't believe such a school could have prepared Barbara well enough for the difficult work she would have to do at Harvard.

Barbara was disappointed that she could not go to Harvard, but she was accepted at another almost all-white eastern school, Boston University. She knew that Boston had a good law school too, so that's where she decided to go.

Barbara's decision meant hardship for the Jordan family. Her parents and her two sisters, who were now working, scraped together all the money they could to send Barbara away to school. But Ben warned Barbara that there would be no money left for her to come home on vacations.

Barbara wasn't worried about money or anything else. She was setting out to be a lawyer. And because she had always been able to do exactly what she set out to do, she knew she would succeed. It didn't even bother her that there were only six women, only two of them black, in her class of 600 students.

But it wasn't long before Barbara found herself in trouble. Most of the other students had come from all-white schools, and many of their fathers were rich lawyers. These students seemed to understand everything in class. Barbara was lost. She did not understand what the teachers—or the students—were saying. It all sounded like a foreign language to her. The teachers didn't even give quizzes. They gave big tests after a whole term. When the first big test came, Barbara had trouble answering the questions.

She thought she had failed that first test. She thought it was the end of her dream of being a lawyer. She went to a movie and sat in the dark, trying to think of a way to tell her father that she had failed.

Barbara didn't find out the result of that test for weeks. She had to think about the test—and what she would do with her life—over a long Christmas vacation that she spent alone in her college room.

When vacation was over, Barbara found out that she had passed the test with a 79. She realized then that the people from Harvard had been right. Her education at an all-black school in the South had simply not been good enough. The Supreme Court had been right—separate schools for black people and white people could not be equal.

Barbara knew she had been one of the smartest students at Texas Southern. And she knew she had an ability to speak so well that people would stand up and clap for her. Now she knew that it wasn't enough to be smart and to be a gifted speaker. She found out that she would have to work hard. She found out that to be a good lawyer, it would not be enough to sound right. She would really have to know what she was talking about. She had to do more than sound right—she had to *be* right.

Barbara almost quit law school that first year, but she decided to stick it out. For the next three years, she worked so hard that she almost never slept more than three or four hours a night. One of her roommates said that often, when she got up in the morning, she would find that Barbara had been up all night studying.

Barbara's years of hard work paid off. She made it through law school. The whole family came to her graduation. That was a proud day for Barbara. She thought to herself, "Well, you've done it. You've really done it."

So far, Barbara had succeeded in the white world, but there were many more tests to come.

Chapter 4

Back to Texas

Barbara Jordan overcame financial problems to open her own law office in Houston.

Barbara could have stayed in the North, where it would have been easier for her to make a career as a lawyer, but she decided to go back home to Texas. She set up her law office in her parents' kitchen because she didn't have any money to start an office of her own.

Most of Barbara's clients—people who came to her for help—were the people who lived in her own neighborhood. She helped people with things like wills, divorces, and real estate sales. The kind of cases she liked best were adoptions of children. She said, "The happiness that goes with adopting a baby or a child brings joy to everyone who has a part in helping to make it possible."

Learning about Losing

By 1962, Barbara had enough money to pay the rent on her own law office, so she

moved her business out of her parents'
house. She had to borrow $500 more for
another reason. She wanted to run for
state representative, and it cost that much
to sign up as a candidate.

By this time, many people in the area
knew about Barbara—the black woman
with a powerful voice and a way with
words. But Barbara didn't have much of a
chance to win the election. In Texas, lawmakers were elected by county. Some coun-
ties had very few people, and some coun-
ties had many people, yet each county had
only one representative, or person to speak
for it. Barbara came from a very large
county called Harris County, which included the city of Houston. More than a
million people lived in Harris County, so
Barbara had to reach a lot of people be-
sides the black people who lived in her
home neighborhood of Houston.

Barbara still thought she could win, if
only she could reach the people. She spoke
before many groups. Everywhere she went,
people seemed to love her speeches and to
want to vote for her, but Barbara couldn't
find a way to speak to all the people of
Harris County. She didn't have the money
to rent huge billboards or pay for TV ads.
Her white opponent did.

Barbara got 46,000 votes in that election. Her opponent got 65,000. She had lost! People told her she should feel good that she had gotten so many votes, but all she could think about was her defeat.

Two years later, Barbara decided to run again for the same office. Nothing had changed. She still didn't have as much money as her opponent, the same man she had run against before. And she still had to reach all of the voters of huge Harris County. Once again, Barbara lost. She was so upset that she thought about moving to another state where she might have a better chance of winning. Instead, she decided to stick it out in Texas. She said, "I am a Texan; my roots are in Texas. To leave would be a cop-out." But Barbara didn't know whether she would ever run for office again.

Speaking Out for Better Schools

By the mid-1960s, black people in Houston were beginning to speak out for better education for their children. There were still separate schools in the city for black children and white children. For years, black people had been angry that the schools had not been integrated.

Working for Voting Rights

Barbara worked to register voters in Houston and get them to the polls in the presidential elections of 1960. It was then that people in Houston and in the Democratic party first sat up and began to take notice of Barbara Jordan. She was an admirer of Lyndon Johnson, who was the Democratic candidate for vice president, and she thought John F. Kennedy would fight for the rights of black people if he were elected.

The white leaders of the city didn't know how angry black people had become about this problem. Many of the black leaders were old, and they were used to telling the white leaders things that they wanted to hear. They always told the white leaders that things were fine in the black neighborhoods. The white leaders believed these black leaders. In 1965, the mayor of Houston, a man named Louie Welch, said, "We have no race problem in Houston."

But there were some young black leaders who knew that there was a race problem in Houston. One of those leaders was a 36-year-old minister named William Lawson. Less than two months after Welch made his speech, Lawson convinced more than 9,000 black students to stay out of school for a day to protest the poor education they were receiving. Hundreds of black people marched through the city to protest school segregation—the separation of black people from white people.

Barbara Jordan stood with Lawson and the thousands of black people who marched to City Hall to demand change. Her voice rang out strongly as she led freedom songs that let white leaders know that black people in Houston were not happy with the way things were.

Over the next two years, Houston finally began desegregating its schools. That is, black children and white children began to attend the same schools.

Barbara was happy about the success of the protest marches, but she knew that the poor people of Houston—blacks, Hispanics, and whites—still needed someone to speak for them. She wanted to be the person to do that, but she wasn't sure how she could ever win an election as long as she had to run in Harris County.

New Hope to Win

Before the 1966 elections in Texas, the United States Supreme Court made some decisions that gave Barbara and other black people a better chance to win.

One of the Supreme Court decisions was that there could be no more poll taxes. A poll tax was a fee that some states charged people for the right to vote. These poll taxes kept many poor people from voting. In cities like Houston, many of these poor people were black. The right to vote, the Court said, should not depend on having a certain amount of money.

The Court also decided that in some states in the South, voting districts were divided unfairly. Voting districts are areas of a state that elect representatives. In Texas and many southern states, some districts had many more people in them than others did. Big cities, where most black people lived, were often included in huge voting districts where there were many more white voters than black voters. And in these southern states, there were many districts that had few people in them, but most of the people in those districts were white. So, most southern states had only white representatives, even though the states had large numbers of black people living there.

The Supreme Court said it wasn't fair for these southern states to divide their voting districts in this way. The Court said that each representative should speak for the same number of people. The idea, the Court said, was "One man, one vote." Each person's vote, the Court said, ought to count in exactly the same way.

Voting Victory

President Lyndon Johnson proposed a Voting Rights Act in the spring of 1965, which was signed into law that summer. He also attacked the practice of poll taxes by taking to court the four states, including his home state of Texas, where the taxes were still used.

The Court did not name Texas as one of the states where voting districts were divided unfairly. But Texas officials decided to change the way voting districts were divided, as other southern states had done after the Court's decision.

So, in 1966, Barbara suddenly found that she was living in a voting district that had never existed before. It was the 11th State Senatorial District. State senators had much more power than state representatives. Barbara set out to become one of those senators.

Victory at Last

First, Barbara had to be chosen as the Democrat who would run in the district. Her main opponent was a white man named J.C. Whitfield. In his speeches to try to become the Democratic candidate, Whitfield appealed to white people in the

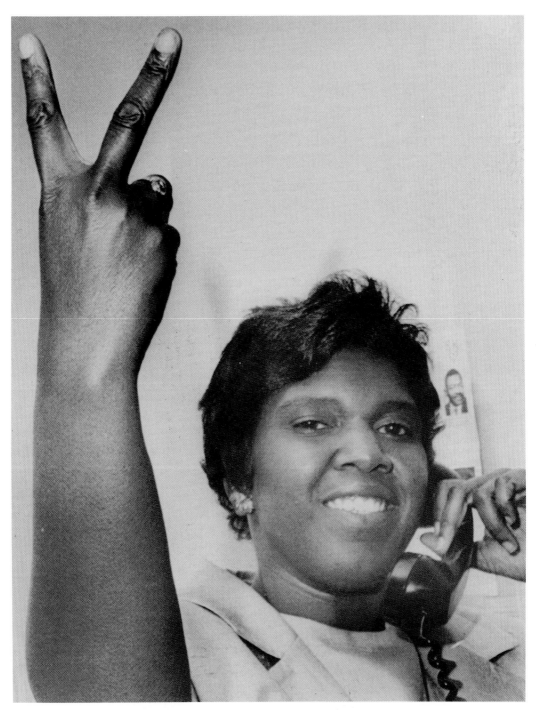

In 1966, Barbara Jordan celebrated her victory for the Democratic nomination to the Texas State Senate. She became the first black woman ever elected to a state office in Texas.

district. He kept asking, "Can a white man win?" In her own speeches, Barbara kept answering him in her big, powerful voice, "No. Not this time. Not . . . this . . . time!"

Barbara was chosen as the Democratic candidate. Her Republican opponent had no chance against her. The district contained most of the black people of Houston, many Hispanic people, and some white people too. But these were the people who knew Barbara and had voted for her before. She won the election easily. Barbara became the first black person to be elected to the Texas Senate in 80 years. And she was the first black woman ever elected to a state office in Texas.

Chapter 5

Working for the People

The state senate met in a great hall. People were allowed to watch the lawmakers from a place called the visitors' gallery. On Barbara's first day in the senate, the gallery was filled with her family, friends, and many of the people who had voted for her. They had all come to wish her well on her first day. When Barbara walked in, they cheered.

The state capitol in Austin, Texas.

Barbara was pleased, but she turned around and put a finger to her lips. She wanted to let the people know in a gentle way that it was against the rules for visitors to make any noise.

Learning the Ropes

Barbara already knew that following the rules would be very important if she hoped to get anything done in the senate. But she was brand new to her job as lawmaker, and she didn't know what all the rules were.

As a new senator, Barbara had another problem. She wasn't like the other senators. Almost all of them were rich, white men. People called them "the good old boys."

Barbara knew that she couldn't be one of the "good old boys." She decided that the way to be the best senator she could be was to work hard. She set out to learn about this new job the same way she had set out to become a lawyer. She studied the laws of Texas. She studied the written rules about how laws were made. And she watched the most powerful senators closely so she could learn how they got things done.

Soon Barbara knew the rules better than just about anybody in the senate. Many senators started coming to Barbara to ask for her advice. Soon, the other senators did not see Barbara so much as a black person, or a woman, or a poor person. Instead, they saw her as a good lawmaker, an equal. Barbara could now get on to the business of using what she knew to fight for the people who voted for her— by making laws to protect them and keeping laws from passing that would hurt them.

Fighting for the Poor

In her senate race, Barbara had promised to use her power to "better the lives of all Texans." But she was especially interested in protecting the rights of poor people of all races. The poor needed someone to speak for them. There were many laws that hurt low-income people and needed to be changed.

In her first term in the senate, she helped to stop a sales tax because it would have hurt poor people much more than rich people. And she stopped a new law from passing that would have kept many poor people from voting.

This law was called a voter registration law. The law Barbara fought against would not have allowed people to mail in their voter registration forms. Instead, people would have had to sign up in person. The new law also would have made people prove that they could sign their own names.

Barbara thought that if this law passed, it would keep many poor people from voting. Poor people usually didn't have cars or even enough money for bus fare, so they wouldn't have been able to get to the registration office to sign up. And poor people often couldn't read or write.

Calls for Black Power—
And Barbara's Answers

Barbara was elected to the Texas Senate again in 1968. That was the same year that Dr. Martin Luther King, Jr., was killed. Dr. King, a black minister, had fought for equal rights for all Americans, especially black people. When he was killed, many black people, mostly students, were angry. They began calling for black power. They meant that black people should fight for their rights and protect themselves against white violence.

Barbara was very sad about Dr. King's death, but she didn't think that violence would make things better. She told young black people to fight back with words, not with bricks.

Some of the people who wanted black power became angry with Barbara. They felt that she had become too much like a senate "good old boy." They felt she was too much a part of the white world. Barbara disagreed with the blacks who accused her of being "too white." She said that if things were going to change, everyone needed to work together. She asked young black people, "What are you going to do to save our country?"

And at a speech before the National Association for the Advancement of Colored People (NAACP), she said, "Throw away your crutches and quit complaining because you are black. Don't belch, choke, smoke, and wish for something to go away. Because when you are finished belching, choking, smoking, and wishing, society will still be here." Barbara would often say to young people, in years to come, "Do not call for black power or green power. Call for brain power."

Barbara used her own brain power to make important changes in Texas law. She pushed through two laws that helped workers. The first law set a minimum wage for workers. The second law increased the amount of money workers could get if they were injured on the job.

Many senators were amazed at the job that Barbara was doing. They started saying, "If you want something done, get Barbara to do it."

Barbara spent six years working for the people in the state senate. Then she knew it was time to move on. Her next challenge would be her biggest.

Chapter 6

The Road to Washington

Barbara Jordan enters national politics in order to spread her message to as many people as possible.

In 1970, the U.S. government counted all the people in the nation. This census, done every ten years, gives the government a picture of how many people are in each state and where those people live. This count of people is important because the number of representatives each state has in the U.S. House of Representatives is decided by the number of people living in a state—the more people, the more representatives.

The 1970 census showed that the population of Texas had grown so much that it needed more representatives in the House. One of those representatives would come from the area around Houston.

Barbara Jordan wanted to go to Washington, D.C., as the new representative from Texas. In Washington, she thought, she would be able to do even more good for the people of her state than she had done in the state senate. But she didn't want to run unless she knew she could win. She asked to be put on the committee that would decide where the state would draw the lines for the new congressional district in her area.

Barbara became vice chairwoman of that committee and helped decide the new district lines. The committee was careful to draw the lines so that the three members of the House of Representatives from the Houston area would be re-elected. The new Houston district would contain Barbara Jordan's home neighborhoods as well as some poor Hispanic and white neighborhoods. These were the people who had always voted for Barbara.

In the meantime, the growth of Houston also meant that new lines would be drawn for the districts that elected state senators. Barbara's old district changed. It still included her neighborhood, but it included many more rich white neighborhoods than it had before. In the new district, it would be almost impossible for a black candidate to win.

One man was very angry about the changes in the districts. He was Curtis Graves, a black state representative who

wanted to be elected state senator in
Barbara's place. Graves accused Barbara of
"selling" that senate seat to the white "good
old boys" of Texas so that she could become a congressional representative.

Graves was so angry that he decided to
fight Barbara to become the Democratic
candidate for Congress.

An Important Dinner

Barbara had lost elections before because
she had not had enough money for post-
ers, bumper stickers, and TV ads. So for
this important campaign, one of the first
things Barbara had to do was to raise
money.

One of the ways she raised money was to
have large parties and dinners. The people
who were invited paid much more than the
price of dinner for their tickets to these
events. The extra money would help
Barbara pay for all her campaign expenses.

Barbara wanted to be sure that TV and
newspaper reporters would write about her
first big fund-raising dinner. So she invited
as many important people from Texas as
she could. One of those people was
Lyndon Johnson, the president of the
United States.

Before he was president, Johnson had

once asked Barbara to give a speech to introduce him. Johnson was so pleased with Barbara's speech that he told her to let him know if he could ever do anything for her. So Barbara decided to ask the president to come to her big dinner. When he said yes, even some of Barbara's friends were suprised. Barbara wasn't. She knew Lyndon Johnson would keep his promise to her.

President Johnson gave a speech at Barbara's dinner. He said, "Barbara Jordan proved to us that black was beautiful before we knew it. . . . Wherever she goes, she is going to be at the top. Wherever Barbara goes, all of us are going behind her."

President Johnson meant that Barbara had already done many important things for the people of Texas while she was in the senate. And he meant that Barbara Jordan was a black woman who could make a difference, not just for black people but for all Americans.

A Hard-Fought Campaign

Barbara worked hard to become the Democratic candidate. She didn't attack her opponent, Curtis Graves, in her speeches. Instead, she talked about all the laws she had helped to pass while she was in the state senate. Many of these laws had helped poor and working people.

Barbara tried to get her message to as many people as she could. She gave speeches at supermarkets, churches, and union meetings. She shook people's hands and introduced herself wherever she went. She worked most days from 8 A.M. until well past midnight.

Barbara's hard work paid off. In the election for the Democratic candidate, called the primary, she won 80 percent of the vote.

In her victory speech, she repeated her promise that if she were elected to Congress, she would "represent all the people . . . black, white, brown, young and old, rich and poor."

All that night, Barbara celebrated her victory with her campaign workers. She didn't get to bed until 5:30 A.M. But at 8:30 A.M., she got up again. The women of Good Hope Missionary Baptist Church were having a tea for her, and Barbara wanted to be there because these people, who had known her since she was a small child, were so important to her.

Barbara ran against the Republican candidate in the November election and won easily, with 81 percent of the vote. But

before she left Texas for Washington, she had to finish her job in the state senate.

The state senate, as a way of saying good-bye to Barbara, voted to make her governor for a day. This would be another "first" for her and for the nation. She would be the first black woman ever to be governor of a state.

That day in 1972 was one of the happiest and saddest of Barbara's life.

It was a day full of celebrations. There was breakfast, a big meeting at the senate, and a barbecue lunch. As the bands played and the people sang, Barbara felt proud.

But one very important person in Barbara's life couldn't be with her on this special day. Her father was ill at home.

In 1972, newly elected Congresswoman Barbara Jordan is sworn in as "Governor for a Day" by Judge Andrew Jefferson.

45

He watched the celebration on TV, where he saw his daughter named "Governor for a Day." Then, suddenly, he became much sicker and was rushed to the hospital.

Barbara didn't tell the people at the celebration about her father. She kept having friends call the hospital and report to her on how he was doing. Then, before a big evening party, Barbara finally went to see her father.

Ben Jordan broke into a smile when his daughter arrived. He couldn't talk very well, but he wanted to let Barbara know how proud he was of her. He was proud because she had used her brain and her powerful way with words to become a congresswoman—and now the governor of Texas.

When Barbara left her father's room, he was still smiling. Late that same night, Barbara was at a party with her close friends when word came that Ben Jordan had died. Barbara said later that he had probably waited to die until her special day was over.

There were still many special days to come for Barbara. Soon she would be famous, not just in Texas, but throughout the nation.

Chapter 7

The Gentlelady from Texas

Once again, Barbara had a new job to learn. In the Texas state senate, there had been only 33 senators. But, here, in the U.S. House of Representatives, there were 435 representatives from 50 states. Here, Barbara knew, it would be harder to make her voice heard.

In the House, each representative must serve on special work groups called committees. Barbara wanted to be on the Judiciary Committee. This committee worked on laws about the U.S. courts and helped to choose new judges for the courts. Barbara thought that this committee would be a good place for her because she was a lawyer.

As a new representative, Barbara didn't have much choice about what committee she would be put on. But she knew one

Congresswoman Barbara Jordan, determined to make her voice heard, managed to become a member of the Judiciary Committee.

Barbara Jordan celebrates her election as congresswoman with former President Lyndon Johnson.

person who might be able to help. She called on her old friend Lyndon Johnson back in Texas. Johnson was no longer president, but he still knew a lot of important people in Congress. He made a few phone calls, and Barbara went to meet a few of the right people. Barbara got her wish. She was placed on the Judiciary Committee.

A Dishonest President

In 1972, during Richard Nixon's campaign for president, there had been a break-in at the national offices of the Democrats in Washington. Five men were caught trying to steal important campaign secrets from the Democrats' files.

Right away, people began to wonder who had hired the robbers. Reporters began to do some detective work. They discovered that some of the people who worked for Nixon had probably paid the robbers. The

Barbara Loses a Friend

In January of 1973, former President Johnson died of a heart attack. Barbara felt she had lost a good friend and that black Americans had lost a friend too. She said, "Black Americans became excited about a future of opportunity, hope, justice, and dignity because Lyndon Johnson lived."

President Richard Nixon was forced to resign because of the Watergate scandal.

next question was, Did Nixon himself know about the robbery?

The newspapers were full of stories about the robbery. Because the Democratic offices were in some high-rise buildings called The Watergate, the newspapers were soon calling the robbery just "Watergate."

All over the United States, people were talking about the Watergate scandal. Everyone wondered what would be discovered next. Then, some reporters found out that some of Nixon's top assistants had known about the robbery and had tried to cover it up.

Detective Work

In Congress, the members of the Judiciary Committee were doing their own detective work. They wanted to find out just how much the president had known about the robbery. The committee had to decide whether the president should be impeached, that is, whether Nixon should be

As a member of the Judiciary Committee, Barbara Jordan worked with important people. Above, Barbara chats with Vice-Presidential nominee Nelson A. Rockefeller.

charged with doing things so wrong that he had to be removed from office.

If the members of the committee voted that Nixon should be impeached, the next step would be a vote by all the members of the U.S. House of Representatives. If the House agreed with the Judiciary Committee, then Nixon would have to go on trial before the Senate. If the Senate found him guilty, Richard Nixon would be removed from office.

Barbara was very shaken up by what the Judiciary Committee had to do. She didn't like Nixon, but he was president! Only one other president in history had ever been impeached. And she didn't understand how a president could do something to hurt his country.

But Barbara also felt it was important to find out the truth. Every day, the committee found out more things that made it seem as if Nixon must have known about the Watergate robbery. There were even some reports that President Nixon had bribed other people to keep quiet about what they knew.

America Meets Barbara Jordan

It finally came time for the Judiciary Committee to make its decision. Each member of the committee was to give a speech on national TV. That way, the American people would know where each member stood. There were 38 members of the committee, and each member had 15 minutes to talk. So the speeches lasted several days.

When the committee chairman called on "the gentlelady from Texas," Barbara was ready. Millions of people all over the United States stopped what they were doing to listen to her deep, powerful voice.

Barbara spoke slowly and carefully. She talked about the Constitution. The Constitution is a document, or paper, that was written a long time ago, at the time the United States became a nation. Barbara talked about the meaning of the first three words of the Constitution, "We the people." She said that back when the Constitution was written, she was not in-cluded in "We the people." At that time, neither black people nor women were allowed to vote. Only white men could. But, Barbara said, people had worked to change the Constitution. Now, she said, *she* was included in "We the people."

Barbara went on to say that she believed in the Constitution. After all, here she was, speaking for the people. She said she wanted to make sure that no one could damage the great government that the Constitution had given all of the American people.

Barbara said it was the president's job to protect the Constitution. But, she said, what if the president himself did not obey the law of the land? Then the Constitution said that the president should be impeached. And Barbara said that it was her duty to do the right thing. Clearly, Barbara felt that Nixon should be impeached.

Suddenly, Barbara Is a Hero

Barbara had no idea how people would feel about her speech. When she walked outside, she was surprised to find a large crowd of people waiting for her. They burst into cheers. Then letters started pouring in by the thousands from people all across the United States. A few people told Barbara she had been wrong, but most people said they agreed with her. Many people wrote about the beauty and power of her words. Many of them asked Barbara when she planned to run for president.

Suddenly, everyone knew "the gentlelady from Texas." Overnight, Barbara Jordan became an American hero.

Chapter 8

In the Spotlight

The committee did vote to impeach Richard Nixon. But before the House of Representatives could vote, Nixon decided to resign. He quit his job as president.

In Congress, Barbara Jordan fought for a Voting Rights Act to make it easier for more Americans to vote.

With Watergate over, Barbara spent more time working on getting laws passed. In the Texas state senate, she had tried to protect people's rights to vote. In Congress, she found she had to fight the same battle. She helped to pass a new Voting Rights Act. This law made sure that people would not have to pass any kind of test before they could vote. It also made sure that in places where many people did not speak English, there would be a voting form, or ballot, in their language.

Barbara Stops the Show

Near the end of Barbara's second term in Congress, the American people had another chance to hear Barbara speak. This

Jimmy Carter, newly nominated Democratic Presidential candidate, along with Walter Mondale, his running mate, salute the Democratic National Convention of 1976.

time, it was at the Democratic National Convention. At this meeting, the Democrats were to choose someone to run for president in 1976.

The huge hall where the Democrats met was noisy. Thousands of people had come to the convention to choose a candidate for president. During all the early speeches of the convention, people had talked and moved around the hall. The words of the speakers could barely even be heard. But when Barbara Jordan started her speech, the hall became completely quiet. People wanted to hear what the famous "gentle-lady from Texas" would have to say. Across the United States, 75 million more Americans stopped what they were doing to listen to Barbara's speech on TV.

Barbara began her speech by talking about the first meeting of the Democratic party, which had been held 140 years before. Every four years since that time, she said, the Democrats had met again to choose a president. She said this meeting wasn't much different because the people had come together for the same reason they always had.

"But there is something different about tonight. What is different? What is special? I, Barbara Jordan, am a keynote speaker."

The crowd cheered for Barbara, the first black woman ever to be chosen to give such an important speech.

People stopped Barbara many times during that speech to cheer for her. Then, she ended her speech by saying that it was important for all Americans to do their part in making America great. She quoted

In 1976, Barbara Jordan gave the keynote address at the Democratic National Convention in New York. She was the first black woman ever to be given that honor.

President Abraham Lincoln, who had said, "As I would not be a slave, so I would not be a master. This expresses my idea of democracy." Lincoln, and Barbara, were saying that it was up to every American to decide what America should be. All Americans— poor and rich, men and women, black and white—should have an equal voice.

The crowd went wild. They shouted again and again, "We want Barbara." As her hometown newspaper said, "They jumped and cheered and clapped and stomped and yelled—and loved her."

Some people wanted Barbara to run for vice president of the United States. She wasn't chosen, perhaps because people were not yet ready for a black woman as their vice president.

But Barbara was so popular by now that she was elected easily to another two years in Congress. She continued to work hard to get laws passed, but her heart wasn't really in it. She missed living in Texas, and she also wasn't sure Congress was the right place for her to be.

It was time for Barbara to go home, where she would take on yet another challenge.

Chapter 9

Barbara the Teacher

Barbara had spent her life learning. She had learned to be a lawyer. Then a state senator. Then a U.S. representative. Now it was time to give to others some of what she had learned.

Barbara Jordan, after a long career as a lawmaker, became a teacher.

The University of Texas offered Barbara a job teaching and Barbara decided to take it. The university had once been an all-white school. At the time when Barbara was college-age, she could not have been a student there. Now the school was proud to welcome Barbara Jordan, a black woman and a famous lawmaker, as a teacher.

Barbara set out to be the best teacher she could be. She said, "It takes a long time to become a good professor, and I intend to become a *very* good one." After many years of successful teaching, Barbara would say that to become the great professor she wanted to be would take "a lifetime."

In 1977, many years after denying her admission, Harvard University gave Barbara Jordan an honorary degree.

Barbara's goal as a teacher was to help young people get ready to take over the country and run it well. She said of her students, "They are my future, and the future of this country."

Barbara was a strict teacher. She expected her students to work just as hard as she always had. She expected them to come to class prepared

Barbara's students loved the teacher they called "BJ." BJ enjoyed them too. At the end of every term, she would invite all her students to her house for a big barbecue. And BJ would always get out her guitar and sing her old favorite songs, like "Money, Honey."

Another Moment to Remember

Barbara taught about government, so she never lost touch with what was going on in the country. People had not forgotten Barbara either. In 1984, one magazine asked women who their first choice for vice president would be. They said Barbara Jordan. But Barbara didn't even consider running. She was too busy learning to become a "great professor."

Barbara did often accept invitations to speak before groups in Texas and other parts of the country. In 1988, she accepted

A Teacher of Politics

Soon word got around the University of Texas that Barbara's classes were the best in the school. So many students signed up that the school held a lottery to see which students would be the lucky ones to get into her classes.

an invitation to speak at another Democratic National Convention.

Barbara had lost a lot of weight since the last time she had appeared on national TV. She was also in a wheelchair. For years, an illness called multiple sclerosis had gradually weakened her muscles. She never talked about her illness except to say, "I am healthy enough to do all I desire to do."

People were shocked by the change in the way Barbara looked. But when Barbara's rich, strong voice filled the hall, a hush fell over the crowd. This was the same Barbara Jordan they remembered. As she told of her hopes for her country, many people's eyes filled with tears. When she finished her speech, the crowd rose to their feet all at once. They cheered and clapped for the woman who made them feel so proud to be Americans.

Barbara Jordan isn't a hero just because she became someone important. She is a hero because she has made a difference in so many people's lives.

Barbara Jordan smiles during the 1984 ceremonies dedicating the Houston post office in her name. Although a national hero, Barbara has never forgotten her hometown.

Goodbye to a Hero

On Wednesday, January 17, 1996, Barbara Jordan died. She was 59. In addition to her longtime struggle with multiple sclerosis, she had also been battling leukemia, a kind of cancer.

Barbara left behind a generation of people—both young and old—who were inspired by her strength and leadership. And, even though she is gone, she will continue to hold a special place in our nation's history—as well as a special place in our hearts.

Glossary

Explaining New Words

committee A special working group. The U.S. House of Representatives has many committees.

Constitution The document of the laws of our nation, it says how the U.S. government must be run.

debate To argue in a formal way, usually by using a speech.

district A geographical division or area for voting.

impeach To charge someone who has been elected with doing something wrong enough to be asked to leave office.

integrated Racially mixed.

judiciary Having to do with courts, judges, and court decisions. The Judiciary Committee of the U.S. House of Representatives handles laws about the courts and helps to choose judges for U.S. Federal courts.

minimum wage The amount of money the law says an employer has to pay employees.

political office A job that someone is elected to do. Barbara Jordan held the office of U.S. Representative.

poll tax A fee charged to vote.

register To sign up to vote.

represent To speak for. A representative is someone who is elected to speak for a group of people.

resign To quit a job. President Nixon resigned from his job when he knew he was about to be put on trial in the U.S. Senate.

sue To go to court and ask for repayment for some injury.

For Further Reading

Bowman, Kathleen. *New Women in Politics.*
Mankato, Minnesota: Creative
Educational Society, Inc., 1976, 47
pages. Barbara Jordan is one of six
women featured in this book. The
book takes a look at important
moments in each of these women's
lives.

Haskins, James. *Barbara Jordan.* New York:
The Dial Press, 1977, 199 pages.
This book is about Barbara Jordan's
life.

Jordan, Barbara and Hearon, Shelby.
Barbara Jordan: A Self-Portrait.
Garden City, New York: Doubleday
& Company, Inc., 1979, 269 pages.
This is Barbara's own story. She
wrote some of the chapters. In the
center section of the book, there are
pictures of Barbara at many of the
important times of her life.

Index

PhotoCredits:
Cover, pages 10, 20, 33, 35, 49, 50, 53, 55, 58, 59: UPI/Bettmann
Newsphotos; pps. 4, 18, 26, 40, 45, 47, 48: The Barbara Jordan
Archives, Texas Southern University; p. 5: Bruce Glassman; pps.
6, 14: The Bettmann Archive; pps. 8: National Archives, photo
by Walker Evans; pps. 22, 54: AP/Wide World Photos; p. 57: The
University of Texas at Austin, photo by Larry Murphy.

Photo Research by Photosearch, Inc.